jazz

TAKE THE LEAD

drums

IMP
International MUSIC Publications

International Music Publications Limited
Griffin House 161 Hammersmith Road London W6 8BS England

DON'T BE A MUSIC COPYCAT!

The copying of © copyright material is a criminal offence and may lead to prosecution.

Series Editor: Sadie Cook

Editorial, production and recording: Artemis Music Limited
Design and production: Space DPS Limited

Published 1999

IMP
International MUSIC Publications

©International Music Publications Limited
Griffin House 161 Hammersmith Road London W6 8BS England

Reproducing this music in any form is illegal and forbidden by the Copyright, Designs and Patents Act 1988

IMP
International Music Publications Limited

England:	Griffin House 161 Hammersmith Road London W6 8BS
Germany:	Marstallstr. 8 D-80539 München
Denmark:	Danmusik Vognmagergade 7 DK1120 Copenhagen K

Carisch

Italy:	Via Campania 12 20098 San Giuliano Milanese Milano
Spain:	Magallanes 25 28015 Madrid
France:	20 Rue de la Ville-l'Eveque 75008 Paris

drums
TAKE THE LEAD

In the Book...

Birdland 5

Desafinado 8

Don't Get Around Much Anymore 10

Fascinating Rhythm 12

Misty 14

My Funny Valentine 15

One O'Clock Jump 16

Summertime 18

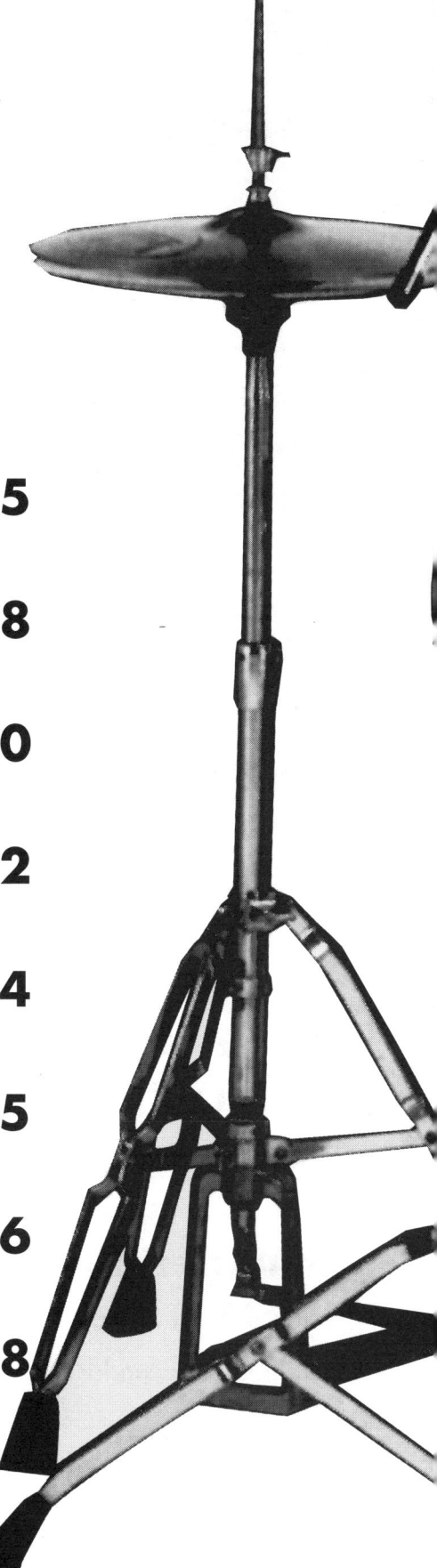

On the CD...

Birdland
Track **1**   Full version
Track **2**   Backing track

Desafinado
Track **3**   Full version
Track **4**   Backing track

Don't Get Around Much Anymore
Track **5**   Full version
Track **6**   Backing track

Fascinating Rhythm
Track **7**   Full version
Track **8**   Backing track

Misty
Track **9**   Full version
Track **10**   Backing track

My Funny Valentine
Track **11**   Full version
Track **12**   Backing track

One O'Clock Jump
Track **13**   Full version
Track **14**   Backing track

Summertime
Track **15**   Full version
Track **16**   Backing track

Birdland

Music by
Josef Zawinul

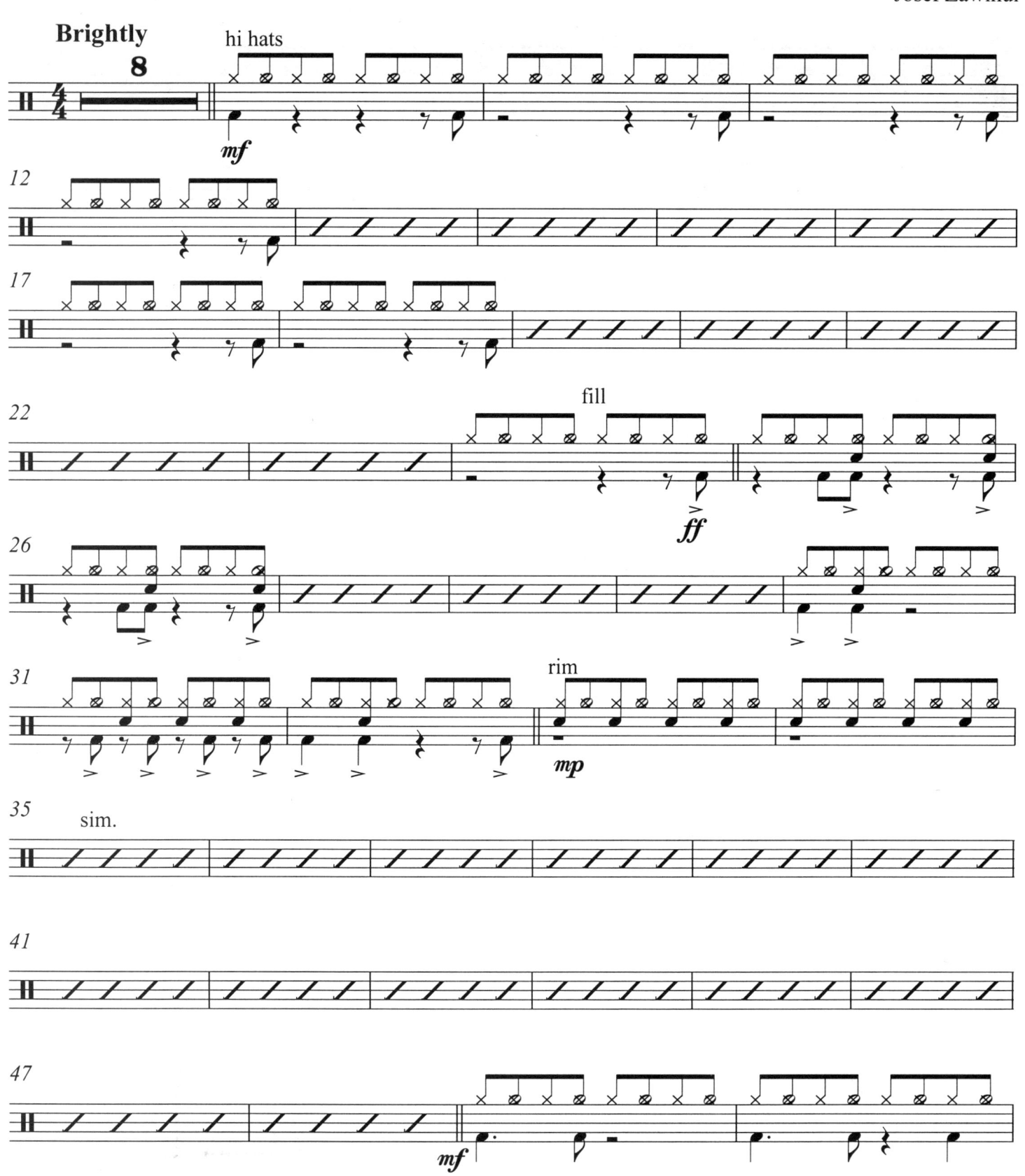

© 1977 & 1999 Mulatto Music, USA
Notting Hill Music (UK) Ltd, London W8 4AP

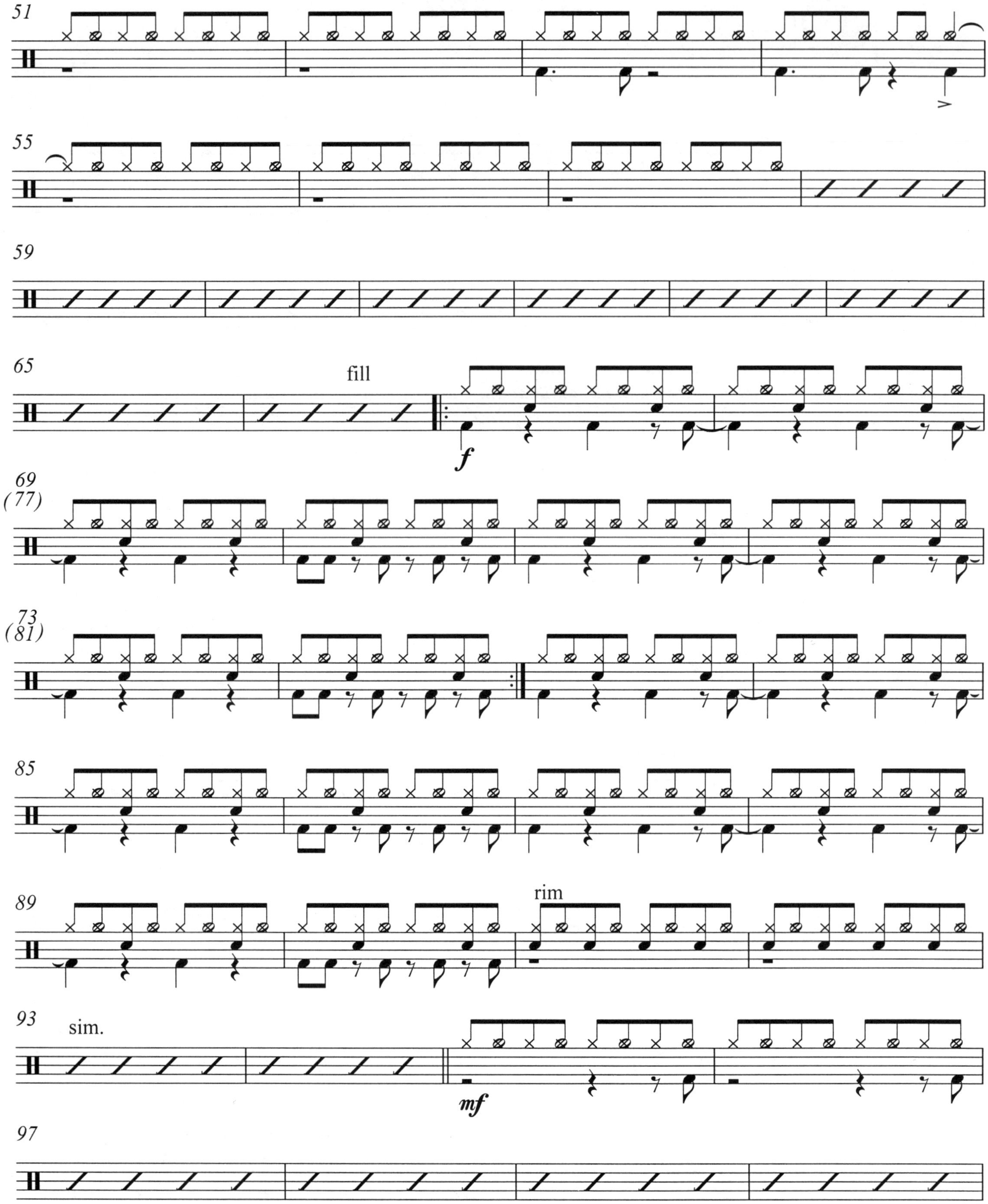
51
55
59
65
fill
f
69
(77)
73
(81)
85
89
rim
93
sim.
mf
97

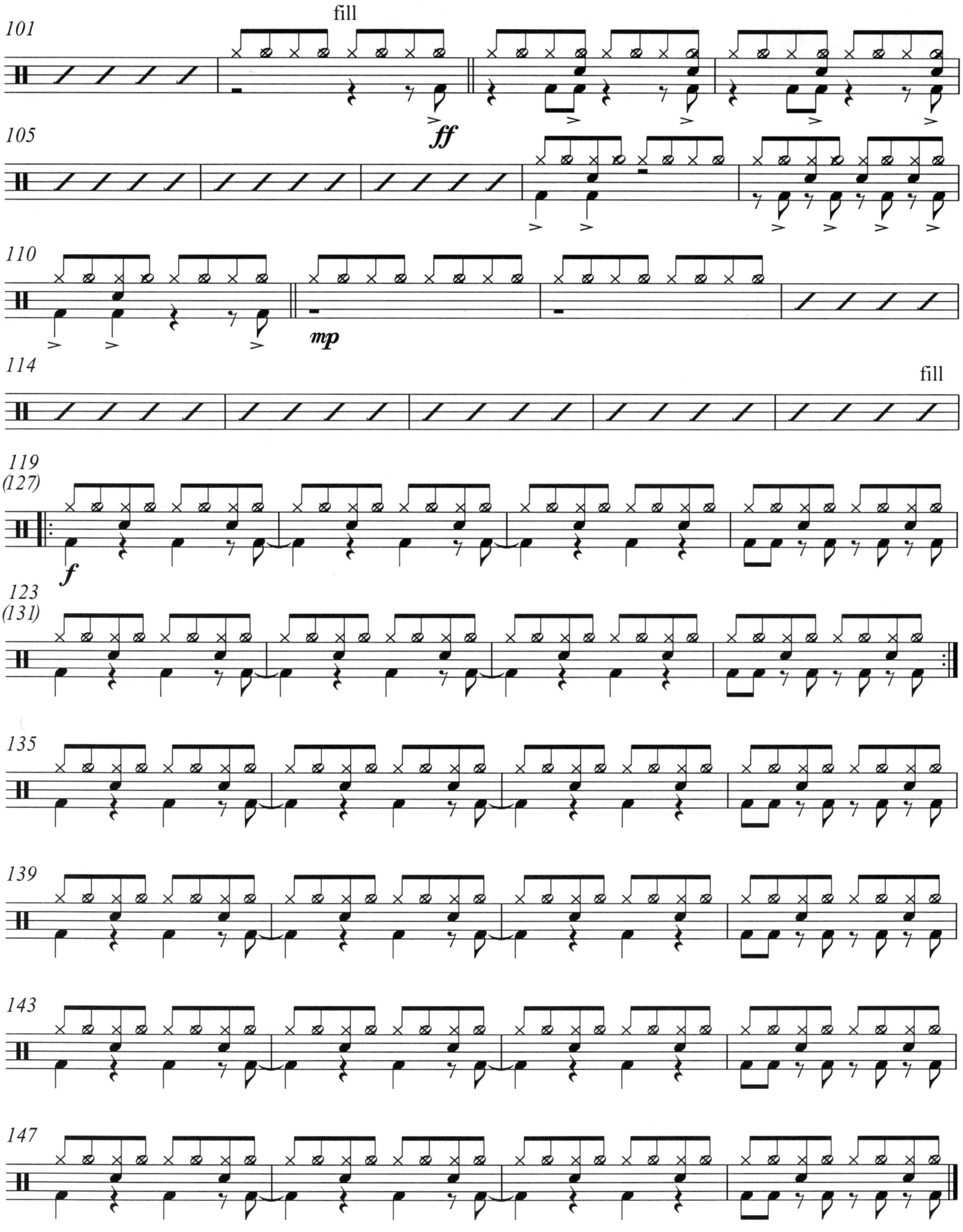
101
fill
105
ff
110
mp
114
fill
119
(127)
f
123
(131)
135
139
143
147

Demonstration

Backing

Desafinado

Words by Newton Ferriera de Mendonca
Music by Antonio Carlos Jobim

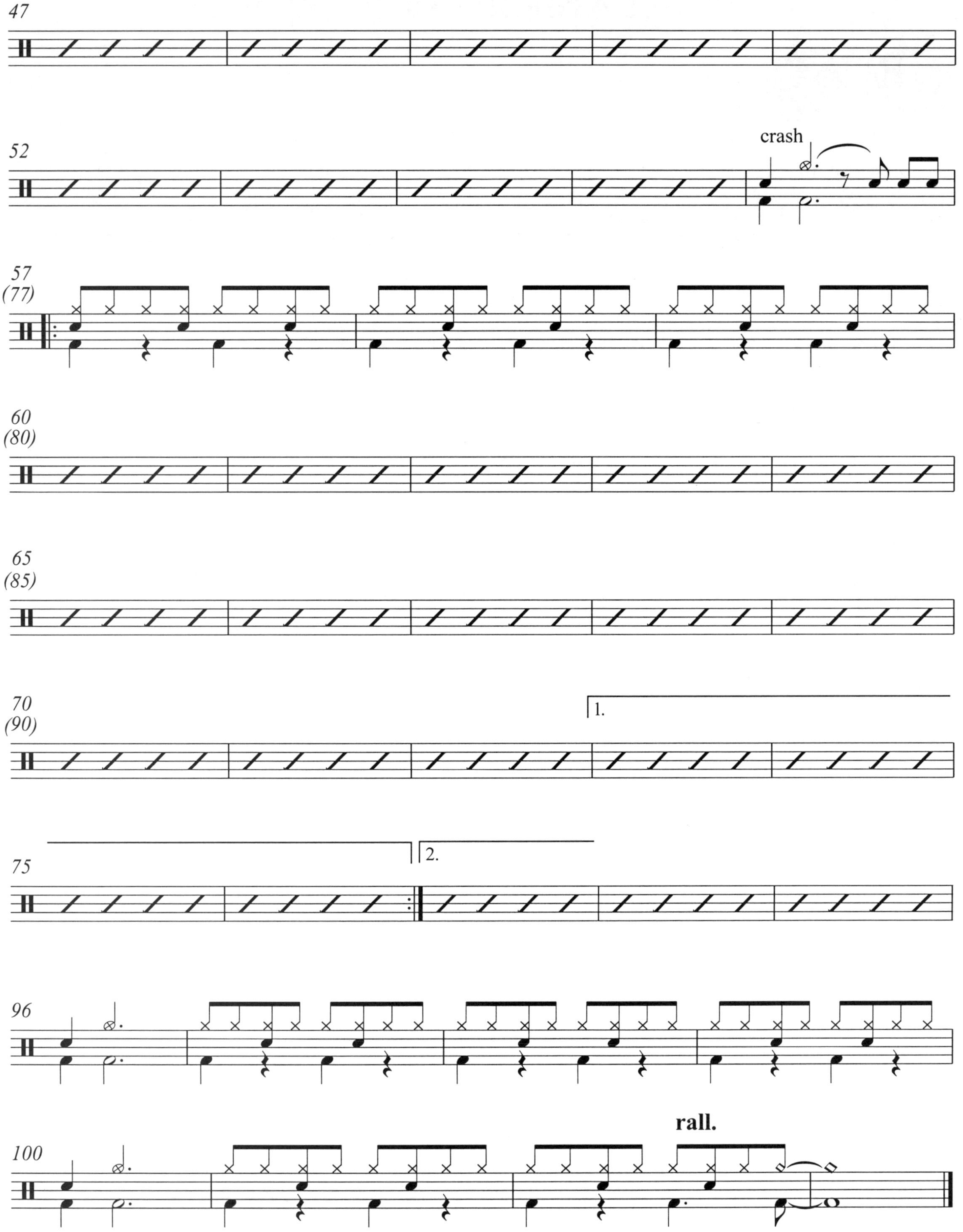
47
52
crash
57
(77)
60
(80)
65
(85)
70
(90)
1.
75
2.
96
100
rall.

Don't Get Around Much Anymore

Music by Duke Ellington

52
fill
rim
sim.
57
63
69
f
75
80
fill
3
85
sim.
90
95
fill
fill
100
fill

Fascinating Rhythm

Music and Lyrics by
George Gershwin and Ira Gershwin

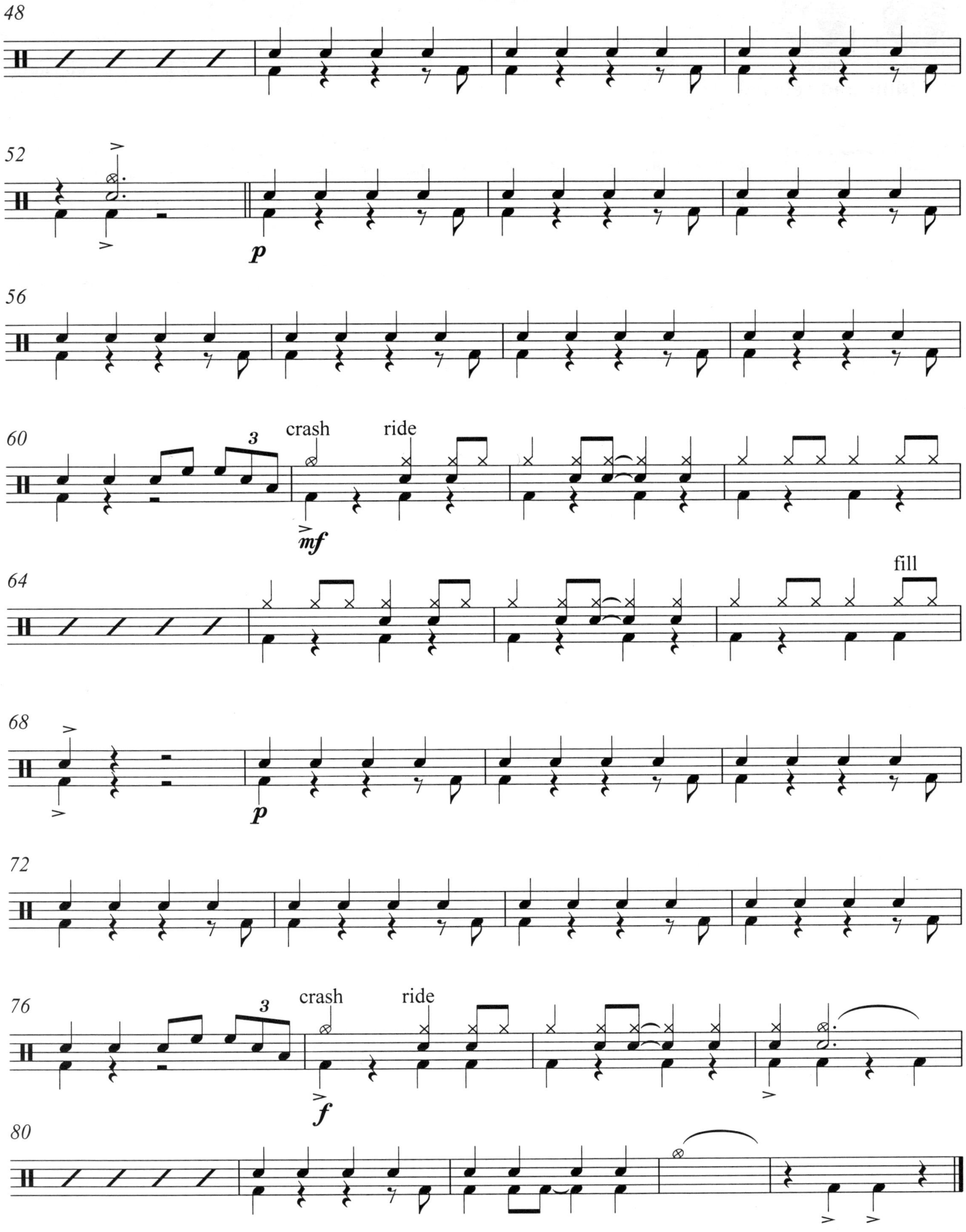
48
52
p
56
60
3
crash
ride
mf
64
fill
68
p
72
76
3
crash
ride
f
80

Misty

Music by Erroll Garner

Slow and relaxed

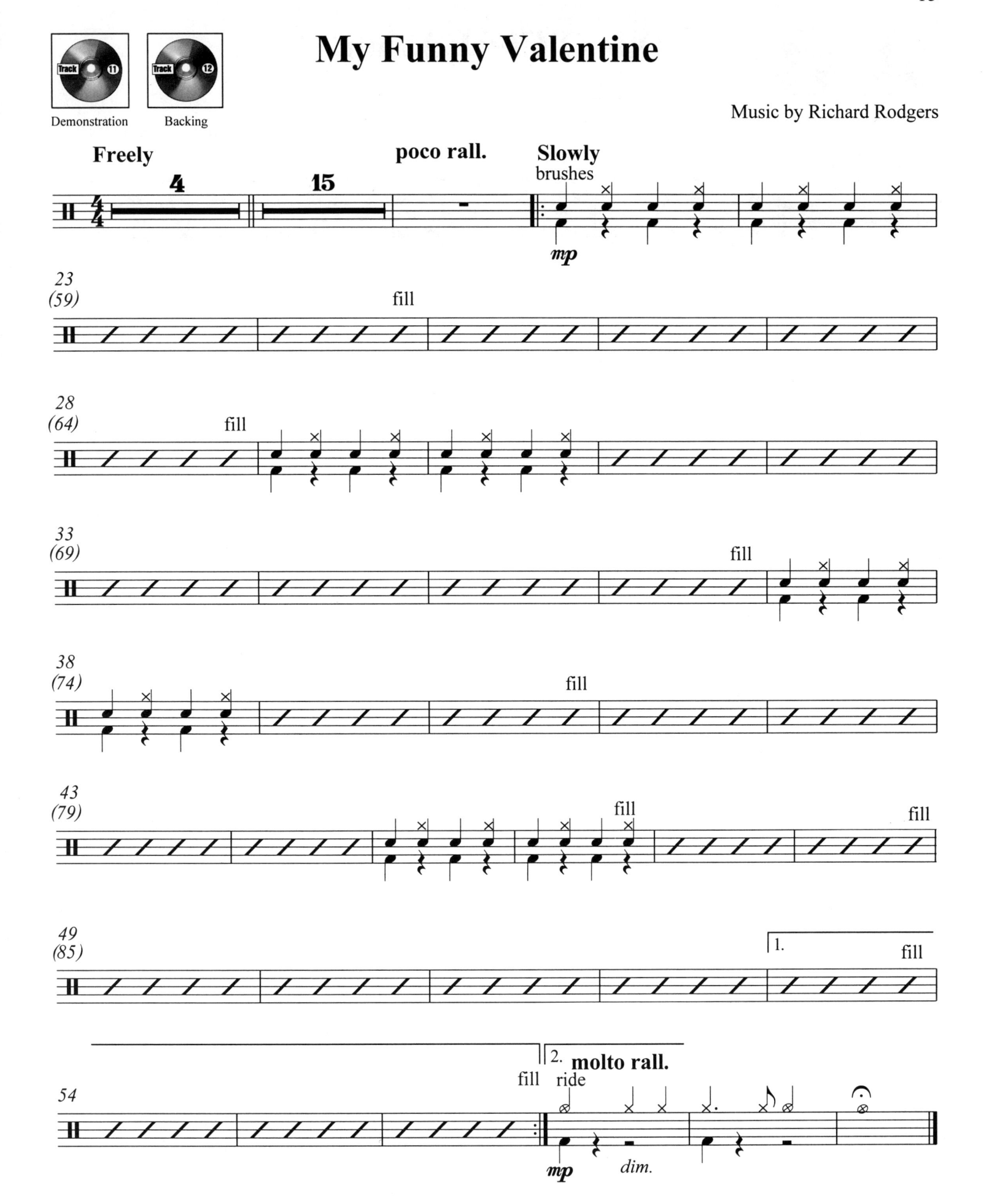

My Funny Valentine

Music by Richard Rodgers

One O'Clock Jump

Music by Count Basie

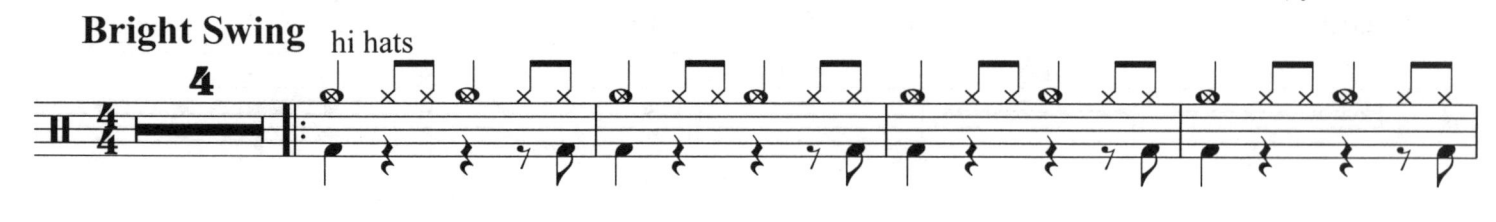

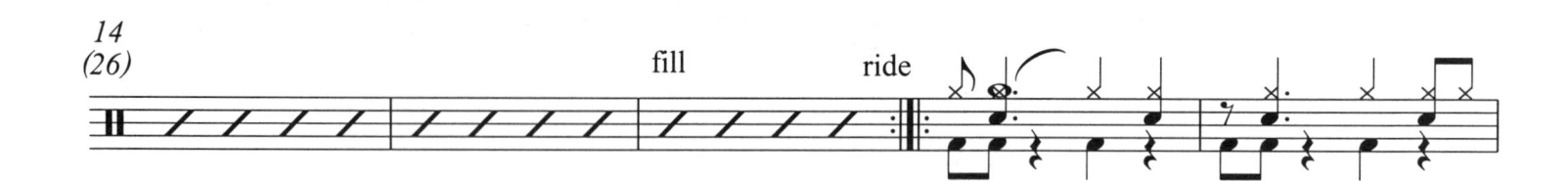

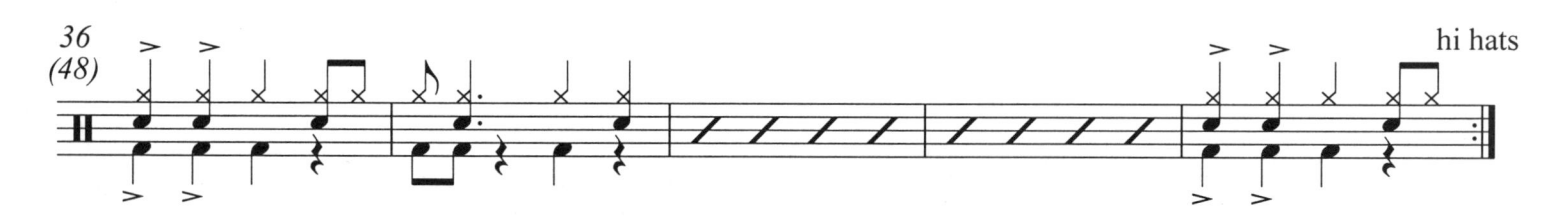

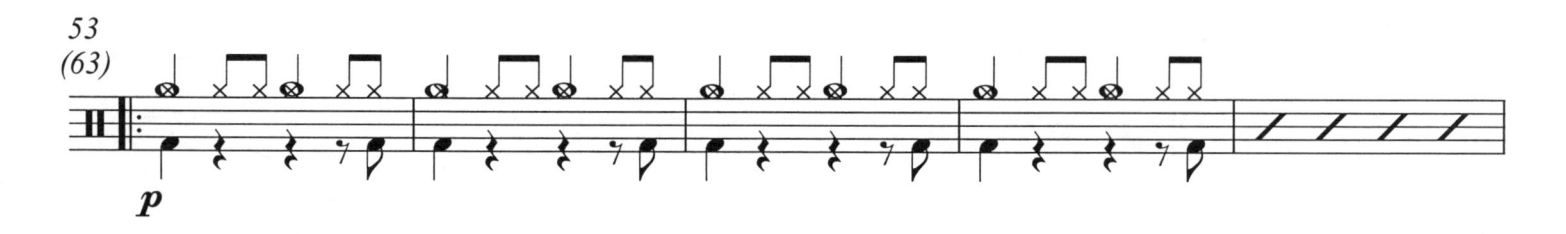

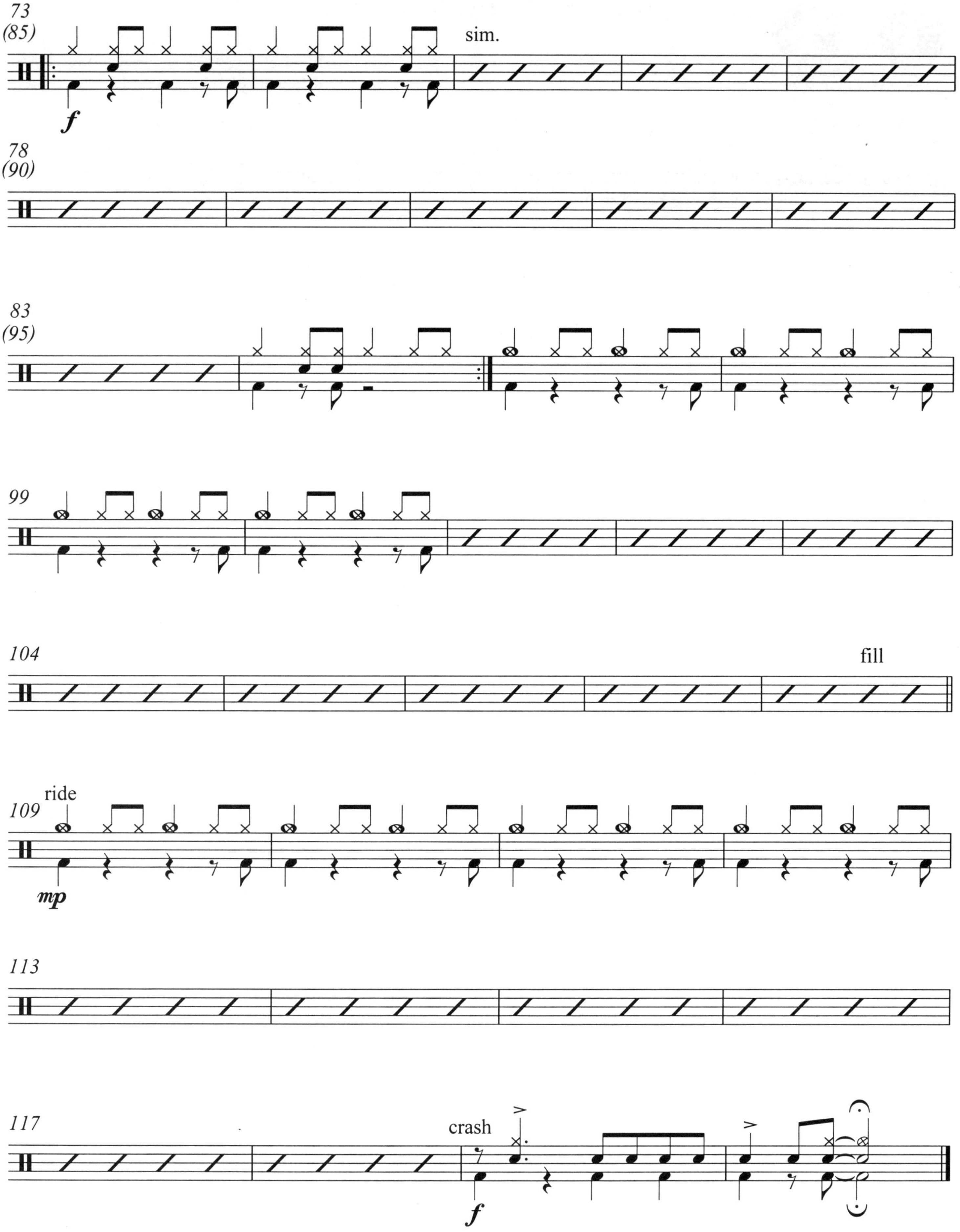
73
(85)
sim.
f
78
(90)
83
(95)
99
104
fill
ride
109
mp
113
117
crash
f

Summertime

Music and Lyrics by George Gershwin,
Du Bose and Dorothy Heyward and Ira Gershwin

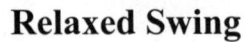

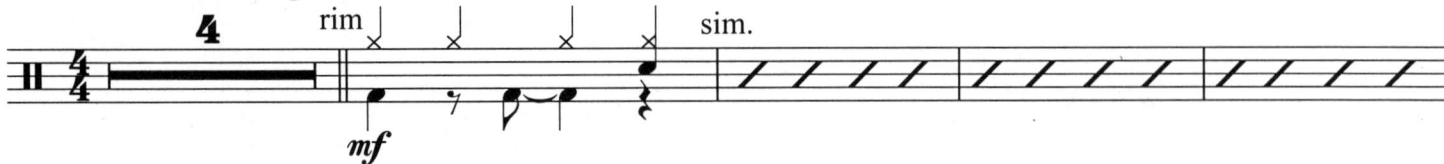

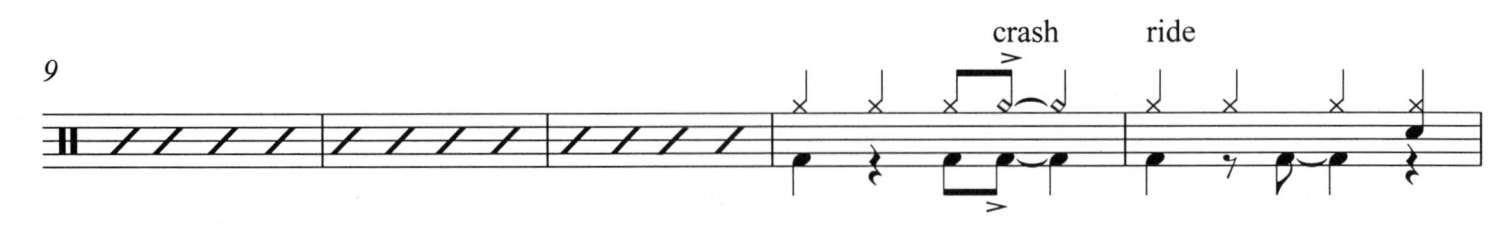

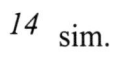

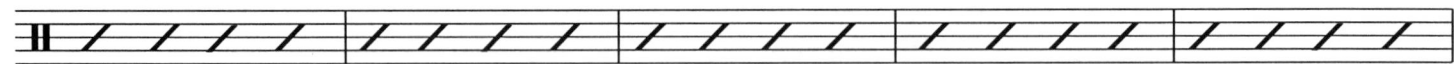

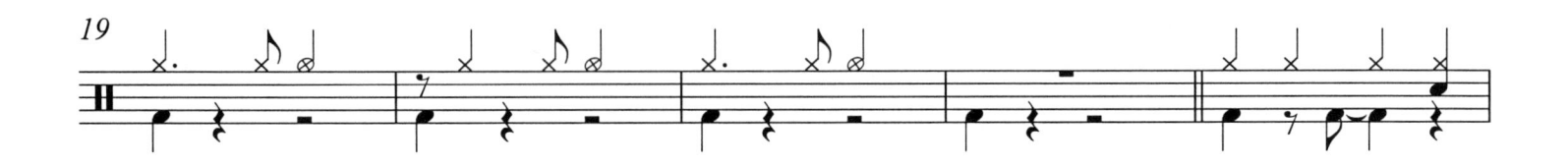

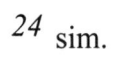

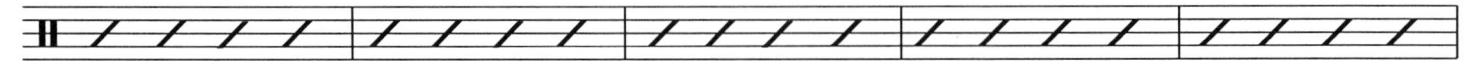

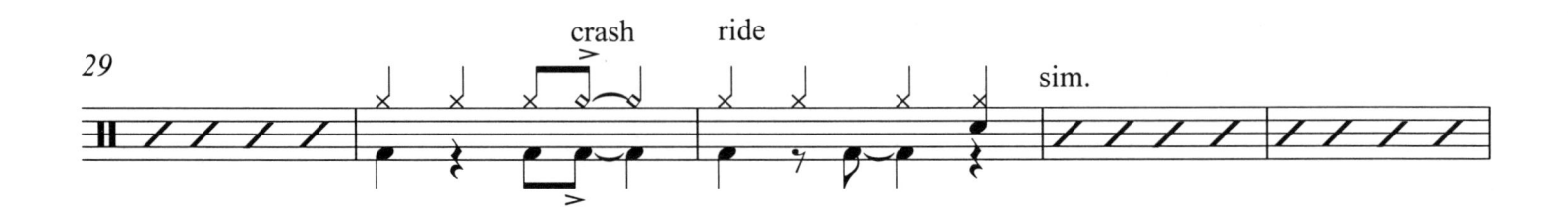

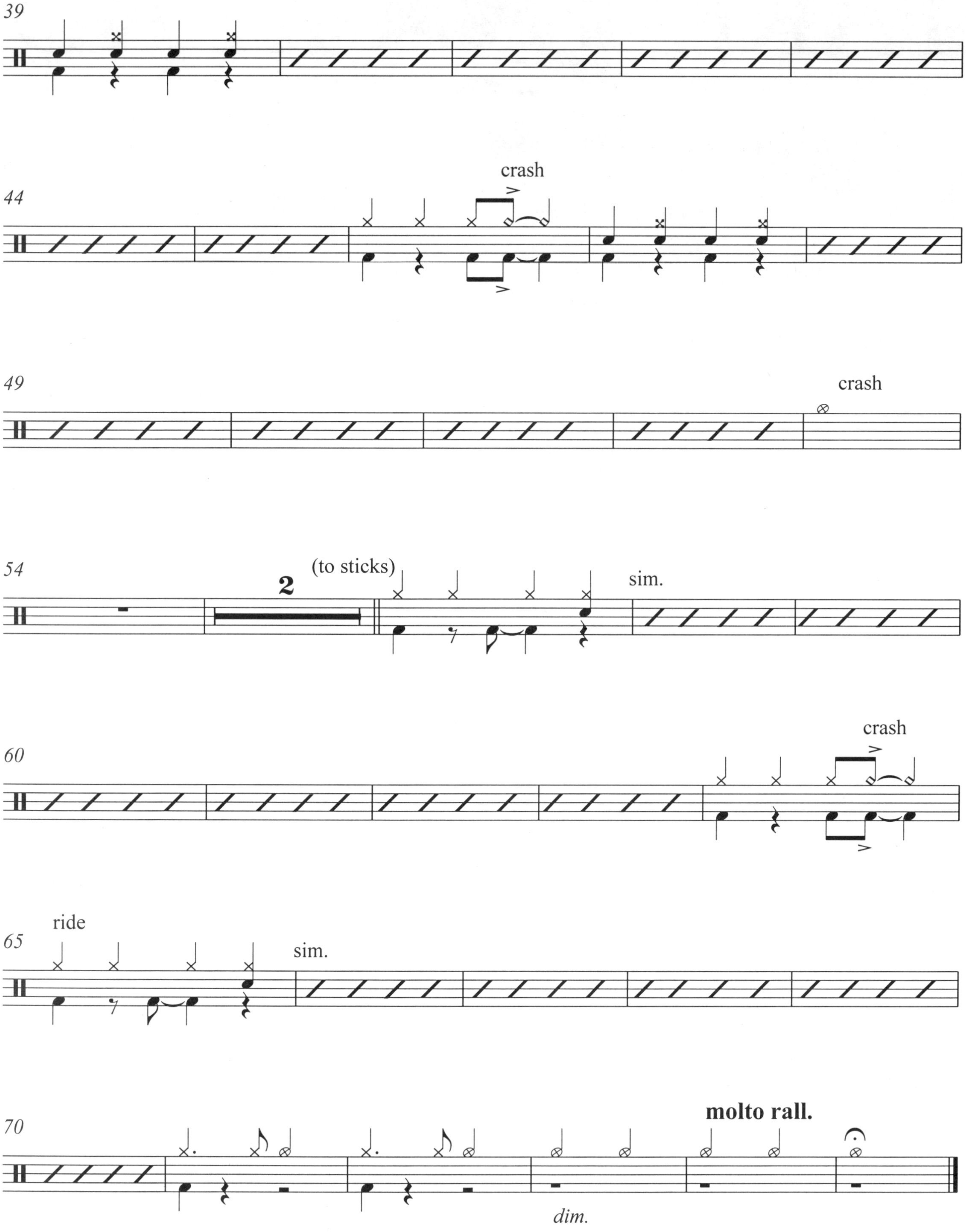

Reproduced and printed by
Halstan & Co. Ltd., Amersham, Bucks., England

You can be the featured soloist with TAKE THE LEAD

Collect these titles, each with demonstration and full backing tracks on CD.

90s Hits

The Air That I Breathe
(Simply Red)

Angels
(Robbie Williams)

How Do I Live
(LeAnn Rimes)

I Don't Want To Miss A Thing
(Aerosmith)

I'll Be There For You
(The Rembrandts)

My Heart Will Go On
(Celine Dion)

Something About The Way You Look Tonight
(Elton John)

Frozen
(Madonna)

Order ref: 6725A – Flute
Order ref: 6726A – Clarinet
Order ref: 6727A – Alto Saxophone
Order ref: 6728A – Violin

Movie Hits

Because You Loved Me
(Up Close And Personal)

Blue Monday
(The Wedding Singer)

(Everything I Do) I Do It For You
(Robin Hood: Prince Of Thieves)

I Don't Want To Miss A Thing
(Armageddon)

I Will Always Love You
(The Bodyguard)

Star Wars (Main Title)
(Star Wars)

The Wind Beneath My Wings
(Beaches)

You Can Leave Your Hat On
(The Full Monty)

Order ref: 6908A – Flute
Order ref: 6909A – Clarinet
Order ref: 6910A – Alto Saxophone
Order ref: 6911A – Tenor Saxophone
Order ref: 6912A – Violin

TV Themes

Coronation Street

I'll Be There For You
(theme from *Friends*)

Match Of The Day

(Meet) The Flintstones

Men Behaving Badly

Peak Practice

The Simpsons

The X-Files

Order ref: 7003A – Flute
Order ref: 7004A – Clarinet
Order ref: 7005A – Alto Saxophone
Order ref: 7006A – Violin

Christmas Songs

The Christmas Song (Chestnuts Roasting On An Open Fire)

Frosty The Snowman

Have Yourself A Merry Little Christmas

Little Donkey

Rudolph The Red-Nosed Reindeer

Santa Claus Is Comin' To Town

Sleigh Ride

Winter Wonderland

Order ref: 7022A – Flute
Order ref: 7023A – Clarinet
Order ref: 7024A – Alto Saxophone
Order ref: 7025A – Violin
Order ref: 7026A – Piano
Order ref: 7027A – Drums

The Blues Brothers

She Caught The Katy And Left Me A Mule To Ride

Gimme Some Lovin'

Shake A Tail Feather

Everybody Needs Somebody To Love

The Old Landmark

Think

Minnie The Moocher

Sweet Home Chicago

Order ref: 7079A – Flute
Order ref: 7080A – Clarinet
Order ref: 7081A – Alto Saxophone
Order ref: 7082A – Tenor Saxophone
Order ref: 7083A – Trumpet
Order ref: 7084A – Violin